UNREAL, BANANA PEEL!

A third collection of Australian children's
chants and rhymes

Compiled by June Factor
Illustrated by Peter Viska

Melbourne
Oxford University Press
Oxford Auckland New York

OXFORD UNIVERSITY PRESS

Oxford New York Toronto
Delhi Bombay Calcutta Madras Karachi
Kuala Lumpur Singapore Hong Kong Tokyo
Nairobi Dar es Salaam Cape Town
Melbourne Auckland
and associates in
Beirut Berlin Ibadan Nicosia

OXFORD is a trademark of Oxford University Press.

National Library of Australia
Cataloguing-in-Publication data:

Unreal, banana peel!

ISBN 0 19 554780 2.

1. Nursery rhymes — Juvenile literature. 2. Children's songs
— Australia. 3. Counting-out rhymes — Australia —
Juvenile literature. I. Factor, June, 1936-. II. Viska, Peter.

398'.8'0994

Typeset by Bookset, Melbourne
Printed in Australia by Impact Printing, Melbourne
Published by Oxford University Press, 7 Bowen Crescent, Melbourne

For children

First, there was *Far Out, Brussel Sprout!*, then there was *All Right, Vegemite!*. Now, thanks to the many, many children (and some grown-ups too) who have sent me their favourite chants and rhymes, we have *Unreal, Banana Peel!*

This book, like the two before it, is made up of rhymes, riddles, jokes and insults from children all over Australia. Some are funny (*most* are funny), some are a bit rude; some are used with a game like skipping or hand-clapping, others are said just for a laugh. Everything in this book comes from children (except for the marvellous drawings, which come from Peter Viska). If you think this is a good book, then give yourself a pat on the back — you and all your friends are the book's true 'writers'!

There are approximately four million children in Australia. Every child knows dozens and dozens of rhymes. To fit all those rhymes into a book would be impossible (and it wouldn't be a book, it would be a mountain!). So don't be disappointed if some of your favourite rhymes aren't in this book, or in the other two: you and your friends could put together your own collection. I would certainly like you to write and tell me about *your* games, rhymes, riddles and jokes. I can't promise another book — but who knows . . .

June Factor
Institute of Early Childhood Development
Madden Grove
Kew Victoria 3101

Acknowledgements

Most of the rhymes in this book come from the letters of those children from all over Australia who have sent me their favourite verbal folklore — although that's not what they call it: they generally refer to their 'poems'. *Unreal, Banana Peel!* demonstrates yet again the rich vitality of childhood in this country. I am grateful to all my young correspondents, whose letters I have answered wherever possible. Their contributions will join the large archive of children's folklore housed at the Institute of Early Childhood Development in Melbourne; some of the rhymes used in this collection come from this archive.

My thanks to Joan Malcolm and Darryn Kruse for their help with filing, typing, and all the other necessary book-making chores.

This book is dedicated to all the

Yvonnes
Oscars
Uyens
Noels
Ginas
Suleimans
Tessas
Erics
Rosies and
Stanislavs

of Australia

Pardon me for being rude —
It was not me
It was my food.
It got so lonely down below
It just came up
To say 'Hullo'.

Cow was sitting on a railway track,
Its heart was all a-flutter.
Train came rolling round the bend —
Now she's milk and butter.

Jenny, Jenny in the tub,
Mother forgets to put in the plug.
Goodness, gracious, bless my soul,
There goes Jenny down the hole!

A dog saw a sausage
Upon the kitchen floor,
The cook saw him eat it
And hit him on the jaw.
Now all the little puppies
Were very sad that night,
They built a little tombstone
And on it they did write:
'A doggie found a sausage . . .'

A monkey stole a frying pan
A monkey stole a door,
The door was off the lion's cage —
The monkey stole no more.

A beetle bought a bicycle
He had it painted black,
He took it for a little ride
With an earwig on his back.
He rode the peddles very fast
And travelled all the day,
He took the earwig off his back
And put the bike away.

Waltzing Matilda
Boos for St Kilda
Up with Fitzroy
And down with Geelong!

Under the bamboo
Under the tree,
Johnny stole a magnet
And blamed it on me.
I told Ma,
Ma told Pa,
And Johnny got a spanking
Ha ha ha!

They tell me there's fish in the ocean,
They tell me there's fish in the sea,
But I buy my fish in the fish shop
So it all sounds fishy to me.

Rain, rain, go away,
Come again another day.

Under a spreading chestnut tree
Stood a vicious bull
Waiting for a lunatic
To give his tail a pull.

Moses was a good man,
His children numbered seven,
He built a little billy-cart
To send them all to heaven.
The road was rough and bumpy,
He didn't know it well,
A wheel came off the billy-cart
And sent them all to hell.

It's a long way to the top
If you want to rock and roll,
It's a long way to the shop
If you want a sausage roll.

I scream
You scream
We all scream
For ice-cream.

It's raining, it's pouring,
The old man's snoring,
He went to bed
And bumped his head
And couldn't get up in the morning.

I eat my peas with honey,
I've done it all my life:
It makes the peas taste funny
But it keeps them on my knife.

The cow kicked Nelly in the belly in the barn:
Didn't do her any good
Didn't do her any harm.

Fat and Skinny went to war
Fat got shot with an apple core.

Fat and Skinny climbed a tree,
Fat fell down the lavatory,
Skinny went down and pulled the chain
And Fat was never seen again.

Cowboy Bill went up the hill
To see the Indians dance.
Cowboy Bill came down the hill
With arrows in his pants.

Captain Cook
Chased a chook
All around Australia,
Lost his pants in the middle of France
And found them in Tasmania.

There was a man and he went mad
So he jumped into a biscuit bag.
The biscuit bag was so full
That he jumped into a roaring bull.
The roaring bull was so fat
That he jumped into a gentleman's hat.
The gentleman's hat was so fine
That he jumped into a bottle of wine.
The bottle of wine was so clear
That he jumped into a bottle of beer.
The bottle of beer was so thick
That he jumped into a walking stick.
The stick broke
Gave him a poke
And turned him into a billy-goat.

My father is a butcher,
My mother cuts the meat,
And I'm the little frankfurt
That runs around the street.

Row, row, row your boat
Gently down the stream,
Putt, putt, putt, putt —
You're out of gasoline.

She stood on the bridge at midnight,
Her lips were all a-quiver,
She gave a cough,
Her leg fell off
And floated down the river.

I love you
I love you
I love you divine,
Please give me your chewing-gum
You're sitting on mine.

30

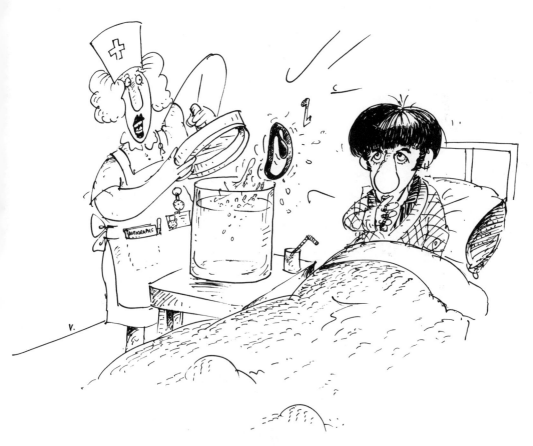

Ringo, Ringo, Ringo Starr,
They put his tonsils in a jar,
They took off the lid to give them some air,
The tonsils jumped out singing
'Yeah! Yeah! Yeah!'

Intery mintery cuttery corn,
Brambly briar and brambly thorn,
Wire briar barrel lock,
Three geese in a flock.
One flew east and one flew west
And one flew over the cuckoo's nest.

Oh, Jemima, look at your Uncle Clive,
He's in the garage learning how to drive.
First he's in the bottom gear,
Then he's in the top,
Now he's on the roadway
Learning how to stop.

Engine, engine, number nine,
On its way to Clementine.
If the train comes off the track
Will I get my money back?

I was sitting on a tombstone,
A ghost came up and said,
'Sorry to disturb you
But you're sitting on my head.'

I love to go to parties
And spoil all the fun
By sitting on the custard tarts
And throwing buttered buns.

Who wants breakfast?
Who wants tea?
Who wants everything
Just like me?

Honey for breakfast
Honey for tea
Honey for you
Honey for me.

Green gravel, green gravel,
The grass is so green,
The fairest young lady
That ever was seen.
We'll wash her in milk,
And dry her in silk,
And write her name down
With a gold pen and ink.

Mothers' Meeting — fathers invited,
Children can come if they don't get excited,
Admission free — pay at the door,
Seats all round — sit on the floor.

Guess what I found?
Guess what I found?
Guess what I found just now?
I found a peanut
I found a peanut
I found a peanut just now.
Where did you find it?
Where did you find it?
Where did you find it just now?
In the gutter
In the gutter
In the gutter just now.
Was it a good one?
Was it a good one?
Was it a good one just now?

It was rotten
It was rotten
It was rotten just now.
What did you do with it?
What did you do with it?
What did you do with it just now?
I ate it
I ate it
I ate it just now.
Then what happened?
Then what happened?
Then what happened just now?
I got a tummy ache
I got a tummy ache
I got a tummy ache just now.

Then what happened?
Then what happened?
Then what happened just now?
Called the doctor
Called the doctor
Called the doctor just now.
Then what happened?
Then what happened?
Then what happened just now?
He said he wouldn't come
He said he wouldn't come
He said he wouldn't come just now.
Then what happened?
Then what happened?
Then what happened just now?

Oh I died
Oh I died
Oh I died just now.
Then what happened?
Then what happened?
Then what happened just now?
I went to heaven
I went to heaven
I went to heaven just now.
What did you find there?
What did you find there?
What did you find there just now?
I found a peanut
I found a peanut
I found a peanut just now . . .

Mother, may I go out to swim?
Yes, my darling daughter,
Hang your clothes on a gooseberry bush
But don't go near the water.

Mother, may I go out to ride?
Yes, my son, of course,
Wear your habit and take a whip
But don't go near the horse.

One fine October morning
In September last July,
The moon lay thick upon the ground
The snow shone in the sky,
The flowers were singing gaily,
The birds were in full bloom,
I went down to the cellar
To sweep the upstairs room.

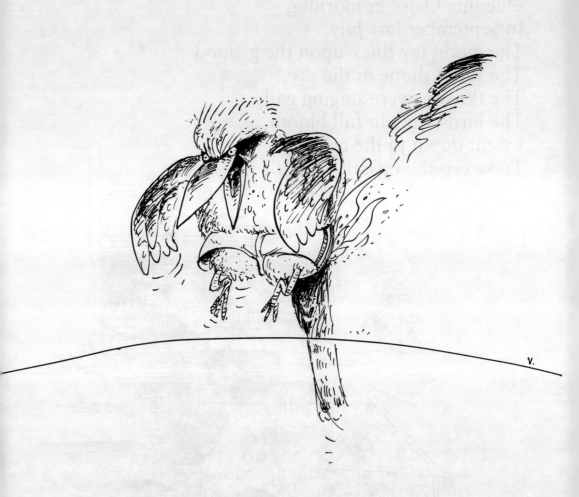

Kookaburra sits on the electric wire
Jumping up and down with his pants on fire.

The boy stood on the burning deck
His pants were made of cotton,
The flames ran up his hairy legs
And burnt his little bottom.

On top of spaghetti
All covered with cheese
I lost my poor meatball
When somebody sneezed.
It rolled off the table
And on to the floor
And then my poor meatball
Rolled out of the door.
It rolled in the garden
And under a bush
And then my poor meatball
Was nothing but mush.

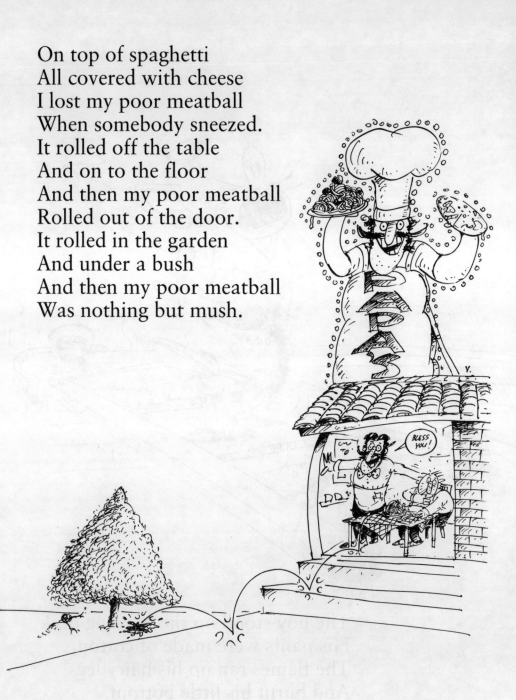

There was a crooked man
Who walked a crooked mile
And found a crooked sixpence
Upon a crooked stile —
And then went and spent it.

Hickory dickory dock,
Three mice ran up the clock —
And fell down and broke twelve legs.

50

While shepherds washed their socks by night
All seated round the tub,
An angel of the Lord came down
And they began to scrub.

Good King Wenceslas looked out
On a cabbage garden,
He bumped into a brussel sprout
And said, 'I beg your pardon.'

Old King Cole was a merry old soul
And a merry old soul was he.
He called for a light
In the middle of the night
To go to the WC.

Happy birthday to you,
Squashed tomatoes and stew,
Bread and butter in the gutter
Happy birthday to you.

Little Miss Muffet
Sat on her tuffet,
Eating her Irish stew.
Along came a spider
And sat down beside her —
So she ate him up too.

Humpty Dumpty sat in a chair
While the barber cut his hair.
He cut it long
He cut it short
He cut it with a knife and fork.

Humpty Dumpty sat on a wall,
Humpty Dumpty had a great fall,
Humpty Dumpty broke his shell —
Poor old Humpty, I knew him well.

Jingle bells
Batman smells
Robin flew away,
Father Christmas burnt his whiskers
Smoking Craven A.

Mary had a little lamb,
Its feet were black as soot
And into Mary's bread and jam
Its sooty foot it put.

Mary had a little lamb,
The doctor was surprised.
When old McDonald had a farm
He couldn't believe his eyes.

Mary had a little cow,
She kept it in a room,
But every time she let it out
She had to get a broom.

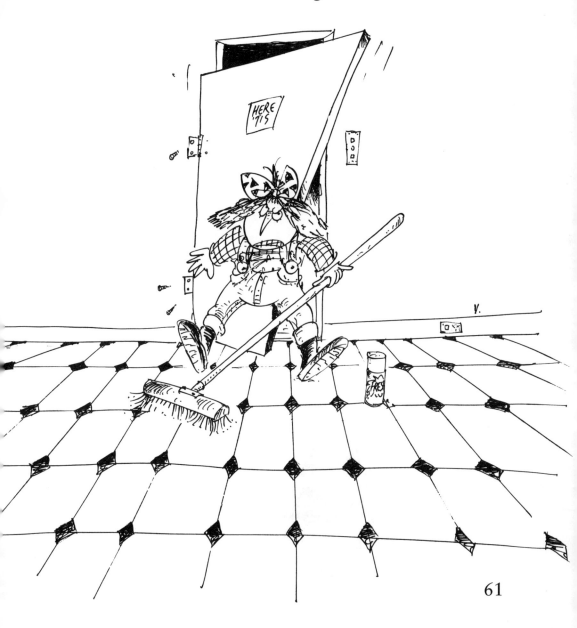

Roses are red,
Violets are blue,
I was born beautiful
What happened to you?

Roses are red,
Violets are blue,
Your dog is pretty
What happened to you?

Roses are red,
Violets are blue,
When brains were given out
Where were you?

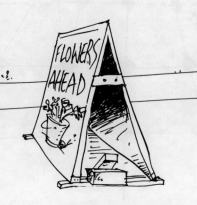

Roses are red,
Violets are blue,
The gasworks stink
And so do you.

Roses are red,
Violets are blue,
Horses that lose
Are made into glue.

Roses are red,
Violets are blue,
Orchids are expensive
Will dandelions do?

Roses are red,
Violets are blue,
I can row a boat
Canoe?

V.

64

The roses have wilted,
The violets are dead,
Sugar is lumpy
And so is your head.

Roses are red,
Violets are blue,
Most rhymes rhyme
But this one doesn't.

Copy cat from Ballarat
Kissed a rat
And never came back.

'You're a PIG.'
'Thank you — a Pretty Intelligent Girl.'

When God was giving out brains
You thought he was giving out milkshakes
And you asked for a thick one.

If your brain was made of electricity
You'd be a walking blackout.

Encore
Apple core,
Kick him out the back door!

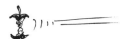

If your brain was made of chocolate
You wouldn't have enough to fill half a Smartie.

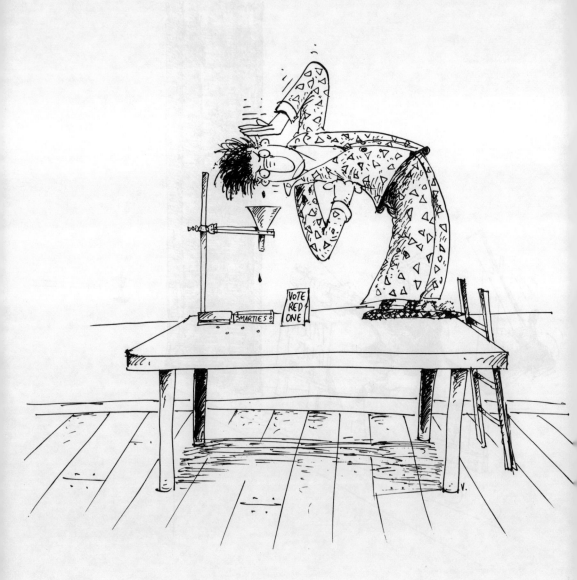

Tell tale tit,
Your mother can't knit,
Your father can't walk with a rhubarb stick.

You can't catch me
You dirty old flea!

You did, you did, you naughty kid,
You swallowed your mother's saucepan lid.

God made the bees,
The bees make the honey,
We do the work
And the teacher makes the money.

Girls run, boys shout,
Dogs bark, school's out.

No more lessons,
No more books,
No more teacher's dirty looks.

No more English,
No more French,
No more sitting on a hardboard bench.

Order in the court,
The monkey wants to talk,
The elephant wants to blow his nose,
Order in the court.

Order in the court,
The judge is eating beans,
His wife is in the bathtub
Shooting submarines.

Order in the court,
The monkey wants to talk,
First one to speak
Is monkey of the week.

'Twas in the restaurant they met,
Romeo and Juliet,
They had no money to pay their debt
So Rome — od what Juli — et.

'How is the milkmaid?'
He said with a bow.
'It isn't made, sir,
It comes from the cow!'

Girl: I got up.
Boy: So I did.
Girl: I went to the kitchen.
Boy: So I did.
Girl: I got out the pig's food.
Boy: So I did.
Girl: I gave it to the pigs.
Boy: So I did.
Girl: The pigs wouldn't eat it.
Boy: So I did.

Early in the morning at half past eight
I heard a postman knocking at my gate.
He dropped a letter and I picked it up,
Early in the morning at half past eight.

Down the lane, a long way off,
The monkey caught the whooping cough,
The doctor said he must have
Salt, pepper, mustard and thyme.

Doctor, doctor, please come quickly,
Mum's just had a newborn baby:
It isn't a boy
It isn't a girl
It's just a newborn baby.
Wrap it up in tissue paper
Send it down the elevator:
First floor, stop,
Second floor, stop,
Third floor open the door
And in comes Mr HOT.

Cowboy Joe from Mexico,
Hands up
Stick 'em up
Drop your guns and pick 'em up
And out you go
Cowboy Joe.

Cowgirl Jill from Broken Hill,
Hands up
Stick 'em up
Don't forget to pick 'em up,
O – U – T spells out.

Doctor, Doctor from over the hill,
Margaret is very ill.
Will she die or will she live?
Yes, no, yes, no . . .

Blue bells, cockle shells,
Eevy ivey over.
Mother's in the kitchen,
Father cuts the meat,
Baby's in the cradle fast asleep.
How many hours did she sleep?
1, 2, 3, 4 . . .

Big A, little A, bouncing B,
The cat's in the corner
But he can't catch me.

Beep, beep, beep for Soula,
Here comes Soula at the door.
Soula is the one who is having all the fun
So we don't want Soula any more:
Kick her out, shut the door.

All in together girls, this fine weather girls:
When you say one, you touch your tongue,
When you say two, you touch your shoe,
When you say three, you touch your knee,
When you say four, you touch the floor,
When you say five, you touch the sky,
When you say six, you do the splits.

Wash the dishes, wash the dishes,
Turn the dishes over,
Shake the mattress, shake the mattress,
Turn the mattress over.

Under the bamboo
Under the tree
Boom boom boom,
True love for me, my darling,
True love for me
Boom boom boom.
When we get married
How happy we shall be
Boom boom boom,
Under the shade of the old bamboo.

Did y'iver, ivir, ever,
In your leaf, lif, loaf,
See the devel, divel, devil,
Kiss his wef, wif, wof?
No I niver, nivir, never,
In my leaf, lif, loaf,
Saw the devel, divil, devil,
Kiss his wef, wif, wof.

Have you ever, ever, ever
In your long-legged life
Seen a long-legged sailor
With a long-legged wife?
Have you ever, ever, ever
In your knock-kneed life
Seen a knock-kneed sailor
With a knock-kneed wife?
Have you ever, ever, ever
In your bow-legged life
Seen a bow-legged sailor
With a bow-legged wife?
Have you ever, ever, ever
In your long-legged life
Seen a knock-kneed sailor
With a bow-legged wife?

My name is elie, elie,
Chickaby, chickaby,
Ooly, ooly, up up up,
Chinese checkers,
Cheese on toast,
Woolly woolly whiskers,
Poke poke poke.

I am a pretty little Dutch girl
As pretty as can be,
And all the boys in my back street
Go crazy over me.
My boyfriend's name is Patty
He comes from Switzerlandy
With forty-eight toes and rings for his nose
And this is how the story goes:
One day as I was walking
I heard my boyfriend talking
To a sweet little girl with curls in her hair
And this is what he said to her:
I
L - O - V - E
Love you
I'll
K - I - S - S
Kiss you
I'll
K - I - S - S
Kiss you
On your pretty little face, face, face.

See see, oh playmate, come out and play with me,
And bring your dollies three, climb up my
    apple tree,
Fall down my rain-barrel, into my cellar door,
And we'll be jolly friends for ever more, more,
    more, more, more.
So sorry, playmate, I cannot play with you,
My dollies have the flu, the mumps and measles too,
I have no rain-barrel, I have no cellar door,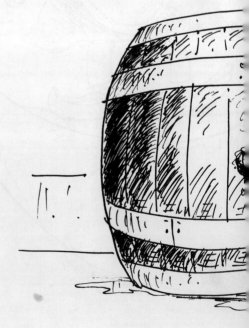
But we'll be jolly friends for ever more, more,
    more, more, more.
See see, oh playmate, I played a dirty trick,
My dollies are not sick, it was a dirty trick,
I have a rain-barrel, I have a cellar door,
Let us be jolly friends for ever more, more,
    more, more, more.

My mother and your mother
Were hanging out the clothes,
My mother gave your mother
A punch on the nose.
What colour was the blood?

Had a little motor car in 1964,
Took it round the corner and slammed into a door.
Caught by the cops and taken to jail,
All I had to drink was ginger ale.
How many cups did I drink?
1, 2, 3 . . .

Eerie, oarie, ickory am,
Queerbie, quorbie, raspberry jam,
Filsy, folsie, Irishman,
Tickle 'em, tackle 'em, bock.

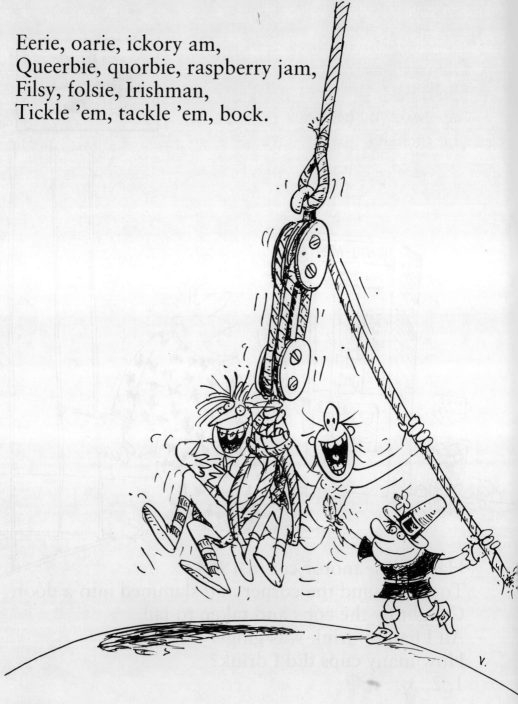

Cat's got the measles
The measles
The measles
Cat's got the measles
The measles got the cat.

R.I.P.
~~PUSSY~~
spotty

V.

One	night
Out	late
Boy	girl
Garden	gate
Father	comes
Big	boots
Boy	screams
Girl	scoots

I 1 a dead horse
I 2 a dead horse
I 3 a dead horse
I 4 a dead horse
I 5 a dead horse
I 6 a dead horse
I 7 a dead horse
I 8 a dead horse.
You must have been hungry!

I C a dog
He Cs a tree
And he does nothing
But P P P.

Bless this bunch
While we munch our lunch.
How now, brown cow?
What's your number, cucumber?
Where's your house, Mickey Mouse?
Cool scene
Jelly bean!

A ring is round,
It has no end,
And that's how long
I'll be your friend.

There was a spider
On the wall,
It had legs
AND THAT IS ALL.

Unreal, banana peel!

For adults

This is the third collection of Australia children's rhymes to be published by Oxford University Press since 1983, and the success of the two previous books (*Far Out, Brussel Sprout!* and *All Right, Vegemite!*) is evidence of the delight with which children have received their own culture in book form.

It also appears that many adults, both parents and teachers, share in this delight, not only because the rhymes bring back the clearest memories of childhood play, but also because they provide a bridge between generations. Adults and children laugh and remember together — and in a culture with forbidding demarcation lines between what is suitable for the young and suitable for those no longer young, that is no small achievement. The little girl from outback New South Wales who wrote, in joyful surprise: 'My mum knows *hundreds* of rhymes!' was expressing exactly this commonality of experience. Perhaps books like these will encourage more adults to consider how much of human life is accessible to all humans, large and small, through the handed-down, polished, perfected yet constantly changing forms of folkloric game, song, story and verse.

Some of the predictions made in the 'For adults' section of *Far Out, Brussel Sprout!* have proved to be correct; others have not. Fortunately, the anxiety aroused by a nightmarish vision of an authoritarian teacher *forcing* children to recite, in proper classroom voices:

> The night was dark and stormy
> The billy-goat was blind
> He ran into a barbed wire fence
> And tore his bare behind

seems to have been quite misplaced. Teachers have generally recognized that children are the experts in this area, and have taken advantage of this reversal of the usual teacher-student relationship to encourage their pupils' linguistic inventiveness. As well, many so-called 'reluctant' or slow readers have made wonderful progress

110

with these books — because they are already familiar with at least half their contents! The positive effect of such confidence-boosting for children who are unsure of their ability to read is recognized by teachers and parents alike, and suggests the value of 'known' material in books for beginner readers. It is also clear that regular rhythm and rhyme help the child predict the words ahead, while humour, almost always present in children's rhymes, makes reading a pleasure.

Fewer adults appear to have considered the profoundly radical implications implicit in the cooperative, collaborative nature of much children's traditional play. For many youngsters, there must seem a marked discontinuity, even conflict, between the competitive and individualist assumptions which underly much classroom practice, and the negotiated rules, strong group loyalty, and preference for non-individual activities which are a feature of their own sub-culture. Some of the books listed in the 'For adults' section of *All Right, Vegemite!* discuss this aspect of children's folklore in greater detail.

As in the previous compilations, the rhymes included in *Unreal, Banana Peel!* come from children living all over Australia, in large cities and in tiny rural communities. Girls and boys have contributed equally (with 'amusement' rhymes particularly, there seems very little difference in the male and female repertoire). Although some non-English rhymes have been collected from school playgrounds, it would appear that in the school environment English is the dominant language, the lingua franca of Australian children at play, even those whose mother tongue is not English. Clearly, verbal play remains a *primary* means of language-learning and social integration for all children.

The 'For adults' section of *All Right, Vegemite!* includes a list of books about Australian children's folklore. Below are a few titles of books in English about children's folklore in other places.

HAWES, B. L. and JONES, B. *Step it Down: Games, Plays, Songs and Stories from the Afro-American Heritage*. New York, Harper & Row, 1972.

HERRON, R. E. and SUTTON-SMITH, B. (eds.), *Child's Play*. New York, John Wiley, 1971.

KNAPP, M. and H. *One Potato, Two Potato: The Folklore of American Children*. New York, W. J. Norton, 1971.

MERGEN, B. *Play and Playthings*. Connecticut, Greenwood Press, 1982.

OPIE, I. and P. *The Lore and Language of Schoolchildren*. Oxford, Oxford University Press, 1959.

OPIE, I. and P. *Children's Games in Street and Playground*. Oxford, Oxford University Press, 1969.

OPIE, I. and P. *The Singing Game*. Oxford, Oxford University Press, 1985.

ROBERTS, A. *Out to Play: The Middle Years of Childhood*. Aberdeen, Aberdeen University Press, 1980.

SUTTON-SMITH, B. *The Folkgames of Children*. Texas, University of Texas Press, 1972.

SUTTON-SMITH, B. *A History of Children's Play: The New Zealand Playground 1840–1950*. Philadelphia, University of Pennsylvania Press, 1981.